She Called My Wife Ping Pong

A Modern Case of Family Violence

Dr Johan Janssen MD, PhD

Copyright © 2025

The moral right to be identified as the creators of the work has been asserted by them in accordance with the Copyright, Designs and Patents Act 1988. All rights reserved.

No part of this book may be reproduced, stored in a retrieval system or transmitted in any form or by any means, electronic, mechanical, photocopying, recording or otherwise, without the prior permission of the authors.

Book Cover by Ven Visual

www.venvisual.com.au

Designed by Red Feather Publishing

www.redfeather.com.au

ISBN: 978-0-6450105-5-8

Contents

PART I   1
1. She Called My Wife Ping-Pong   2
2. Reasonable Concerns   9
3. Tone   15
PART II   18
4. Frequency   19
5. Urgency   22
6. Documentation   25
7. Sleep   28
PART III   31
8. File Names   32

9.	Neutral Language	35
10.	The Bundle	38
11.	Translation	41

PART IV · 44

12.	The Building	45
13.	Orders Pending	50
14.	Silence	53

PART V · 56

15.	Parents	57
16.	Siblings	60

PART VI · 63

17.	Muscle Memory	64
18.	The Child	66
19.	Identity Without Urgency	68
20.	Grief	71

PART VII · 73

21.	Ping-Pong Revisited	74

22. The Last Message	77
Author's Note	79
Dedication	81
Epigraph	82
Author Bio	83

PART I
OPENING VOLLEYS

1

She Called My Wife Ping-Pong

The message arrived before morning had fully committed to itself.

This was important. Morning, I would later realize, had not yet had time to apply its makeup. The light was still undecided. The kettle had not boiled. The day had not yet acquired its excuses.

The phone vibrated once on the bedside table. Not urgently. Not insistently. Just enough to suggest relevance.

I did not pick it up right away. I lay there for a moment, listening to the quiet machinery of the house—pipes adjusting to temperature, the refrigerator performing its low, existential hum. My wife breathed evenly beside me, a sound so ordinary it felt deliberate.

Then the phone vibrated again.

I reached for it with the cautious intimacy reserved for things that have bitten you before.

The message was short. This was unusual. Zola tended toward length, toward elaboration, toward paragraphs that implied legal counsel even when none was present. Brevity suggested either efficiency or intent.

I read it once.

Then again.

Then aloud, because sometimes language reveals itself when spoken, like a chemical that only reacts to air.

DR JOHAN JANSSEN MD, PHD

Your wife looks like a ping-pong ball

SHE CALLED MY WIFE PING PONG

No punctuation.
No greeting.
No explanation.

Just the sentence, perfectly balanced between childishness and precision.

I stared at the screen, waiting for the rest of it to load. Phones had trained us to expect continuation. Three dots. A follow-up. Context.

Nothing arrived.

My wife rolled onto her side and opened one eye.

"What is it?" she asked, in the tone of someone who had learned to distinguish between inconvenience and catastrophe.

"She says you look like a ping-pong ball," I said.

There was a pause. Not shock. Not offense. Calculation.

"Do you think that's metaphorical," she asked, "or is she commenting on surface area?"

This was my wife's gift: the ability to treat absurdity as a data point rather than a threat. She sat up, reached for her water and considered the insult as if it were a crossword clue.

"Because if it's surface area," she added, "I'd like clarification. A ping-pong ball is quite efficient."

I laughed. This, too, would later reveal itself as important.

Laughter is how these things get through the door.

At the time, I did not yet understand that the sentence had not been sent to insult my wife. My wife was incidental. The target was the space between us—our bedroom, the atmosphere, the shared assumption that mornings were neutral territory.

The insult was not an attack. It was a probe.

Zola was checking whether she still had access.

I did not reply.

This was not strategy. It was instinct. I had learned, through experience, that responses were invitations. Even silence, when correctly interpreted, could be read as an admission of guilt. But at that moment, I simply did not know how to answer a sentence that did not pretend to be about anything.

The kettle clicked off in the kitchen. Toast burned faintly. The day, having overheard the exchange, proceeded anyway.

Later, I would try to remember whether this had been the first time she spoke about my wife at all. It wasn't. There had been others. Comparisons. Observations. Evaluations delivered as facts.

But this was the first time the comment arrived stripped of pretence. No concern. No justification. No parental framing.

Just the sentence.

Ping-pong.

I carried it with me into the shower, where it echoed against tile. I repeated it silently while brushing my teeth, curious whether repetition would drain it of meaning.

It did not.

At work, I found myself imagining a ping-pong ball on my desk. White. Hollow. Designed for impact. Designed to bounce indefinitely as long as someone kept hitting it.

DR JOHAN JANSSEN MD, PHD

The metaphor, I would eventually realize, had been unintentional yet exact.

2

Reasonable Concerns

At noon, another message arrived. Longer this time. Administrative. About schedules. About responsibility. About the child.

This, too, was important.

The insult had not replaced communication. It had been inserted into it. Violence, I would later learn, does not interrupt routine. It embeds itself inside it.

By evening, the morning's message had already begun to feel strangely ordinary. This was the most dangerous part—not the sting, but the speed with which it faded into background noise.

At dinner, my wife asked whether I planned to respond.

"I don't know what to say," I told her.

"That's probably the point," she said.

She was right, though neither of us yet knew how thoroughly.

That night, as I placed my phone on the bedside table, face down, I felt the first faint tightening in my chest. Not fear. Anticipation.

Somewhere in the house's quiet systems, something had shifted.

The game had begun.

By lunchtime, the insult had been absorbed into the day.

This was its real achievement.

It hadn't lingered like a wound. It hadn't demanded confrontation. It had simply taken up residence, like a smell you only notice when you leave the room and return later.

At 2:14 p.m., another message arrived.

This one had paragraphs.

Paragraphs, in Zola's style, were always a relief. Paragraphs meant structure. Paragraphs meant intention. Paragraphs meant she was once again being reasonable.

I'm concerned about the tone in your household.

The child has mentioned feeling unsettled.

We need to talk about boundaries.

Boundaries.

A word she loved.

A word she used the way other people use weapons.

I reread the message carefully, as if it were a contract written in disappearing ink. The insult from the morning hovered nearby, unstated but intact, like an annotation only I could see.

I typed a reply.

Deleted it.

Typed another.

Deleted that too.

My wife watched this process with the detached interest of someone observing a complicated ritual they had no intention of learning.

"You know," she said, "in normal families, people say things like *hello*."

"I don't want to escalate," I said.

This was another phrase I would come to recognize as dangerous. *Not wanting to escalate* had become my primary moral identity. I wore it like a badge. It allowed me to endure things quietly while congratulating myself on restraint.

I sent a neutral response. Carefully calibrated. Polite. Informational.

It did not matter.

Ten minutes later, my phone vibrated again.

Your defensiveness is concerning.

This is exactly the kind of environment I worry about.

Defensive.

Another favourite.

Defensive meant any response that was not submission. Defensive meant evidence. Defensive meant memory.

SHE CALLED MY WIFE PING PONG

By mid-afternoon, the day had developed a rhythm. Message. Pause. Reply. Correction. Escalation framed as concern.

I began to understand something essential: This was not communication.

It was calibration.

She was adjusting me.

That evening, while cooking dinner, I felt the subtle tightening begin—the sense that my time was no longer my own. That any moment could be requisitioned, interpreted, repurposed as evidence of character.

My wife asked whether we should block her number.

"No," I said immediately.

The speed of my answer surprised both of us.

Blocking would look hostile. Blocking would look guilty. Blocking would suggest something to hide.

Silence was never neutral. Silence was always read.

Later, lying in bed, I scrolled back to the morning's message. Ping-pong. I tried to see it as ridiculous. I tried to laugh again.

But something had shifted.

The insult was not isolated. It was connective tissue.

It linked to something older. A way of speaking that placed people in categories: competent, unstable, inappropriate, concerning.

I turned the phone face down and stared at the ceiling, aware of a sensation I could not yet name.

Not fear.

Not anger.

Preparation.

3

Tone

Zola had strong opinions about tone.

Tone, according to her, was everything. Tone determined safety. Tone determined intent. Tone was how she measured morality.

This gave her an advantage.

Tone is invisible. Tone cannot be quoted. Tone cannot be disproved. Tone exists entirely in the interpretation of the listener, which meant she controlled it absolutely.

Your tone is aggressive.
Your tone is inappropriate.
The tone of your household is alarming.
Household tone.

I pictured it as wallpaper. Something you selected without thinking and then lived inside for years.

When I asked for examples, she accused me of being evasive.

When I apologized, she accused me of being manipulative.

When I stopped responding immediately, she accused me of neglect.

The child moved between households during this period with the quiet adaptability of someone who had learned that adults were unreliable narrators.

She asked questions carefully.

She watched reactions.

She learned when to speak and when not to.

One afternoon, while drawing, she said, "Mummy says you're angry in messages."

"I'm not angry," I said.

She nodded, unconvinced. Children trust patterns more than assurances.

That night, I reread weeks of messages. Not for content—for tone. I began to see what she meant, or rather, what she needed to mean.

SHE CALLED MY WIFE PING PONG

Tone was how she kept me busy.

As long as we were discussing *how* I spoke, we were never discussing *what* she said.

The insult about my wife no longer appeared in writing. It didn't need to. Its work was done.

From then on, everything was about atmosphere. Environment. Emotional safety.

She had learned to weaponize abstraction.

My wife, ever practical, suggested documenting everything.

"This isn't normal," she said.

I bristled.

Normal was another thing I was reluctant to invoke. Normal suggested standards. Standards suggested judgment. Judgment suggested escalation.

Still, I began saving messages. Screenshots at first. Then folders.

I told myself it was temporary. Just until things settled.

They did not settle.

They multiplied.

PART II
THE NOISE

4

Frequency

The problem was not what she said.

The problem was how often.

This distinction took me a long time to understand.

If someone insults you once, you have a story.

If someone insults you every day, you have weather.

Zola messaged the way people breathed—automatically, rhythmically, without considering whether anyone else required oxygen. Mornings began with updates. Afternoons brought corrections.

Evenings delivered reflections, often framed as disappointment.

I'm still thinking about your response earlier.

I don't feel reassured.

We need to address this.

Address was another favourite word. Address implied something was wrong without specifying what. Address created obligation without conclusion.

By the third week, I noticed my body reacting before my mind. My shoulders tightened at the sound of vibration. My jaw clenched pre-emptively, like a boxer waiting for the bell.

Sleep became lighter. I woke before alarms. Sometimes I woke convinced I had missed something—an accusation, a demand, a tone miscalculation.

My wife began asking whether I had eaten.

This, too, was data.

One evening, while we watched television, my phone buzzed six times in ten minutes.

SHE CALLED MY WIFE PING PONG

The messages were not urgent. They were reflective.

I don't like how this feels.
I'm trying to be reasonable.
I hope you can meet me halfway.

Halfway to where was never specified.

I typed a response. Deleted it. Typed another.

My wife muted the television.

"You're not here," she said, gently.

She was right. I was somewhere else—inside a conversation that had no physical location but consumed real time. A conversation that could not be paused or completed.

I turned the phone face down.

It buzzed again, immediately, as if offended by the gesture.

Later, in bed, I scrolled through the thread. Hundreds of messages. Thousands of words. All circling the same absence: resolution.

I began to suspect that resolution was not the goal.

5
Urgency

Urgency arrived disguised as care.

I need an answer now.

This can't wait.

The child's wellbeing is at stake.

These messages arrived at odd hours. Early mornings. Late nights. Weekends. Holidays.

Urgency flattened context. It erased nuance. It turned every moment into a test.

If I replied immediately, I was reactive.

If I delayed, I was irresponsible.

The correct response time, I learned, was always *just before* I responded.

One night, my phone buzzed at 2:47 a.m.

SHE CALLED MY WIFE PING PONG

Are you awake?
I'm worried.

I stared at the screen, heart racing, aware that my reaction—or lack of one—would be interpreted regardless of intent.

I did not reply.

In the morning, there were twelve new messages.

Concern had curdled into accusation.

Your silence speaks volumes.
This is exactly what I mean.
I'm documenting this.

Documenting.

She said it casually, as if it were a shared hobby.

That was when I realized she had already built her version of the story. My participation was optional.

The urgency was not about the child. It was about access.

She needed to know she could still reach me at any time. That she could still interrupt my sleep, my meals, my marriage, my thoughts.

That night, while brushing my teeth, I caught my reflection rehearsing explanations.

This, I understood dimly, was how it worked.

You begin to narrate yourself in advance.

6

Documentation

Documentation began as a suggestion.

My wife said it gently, as if recommending a new brand of detergent.

"Maybe you should save these," she said. "Just in case."

Just in case is how ordinary people step into extraordinary situations. No one documents because they expect catastrophe. They document because they hope to avoid it.

I started with screenshots. The occasional one, when something felt particularly sharp or strange. The insults were rare now. She had learned better. Insults were inefficient. What she preferred was implication.

I'm worried about the kind of language you're modelling.

I don't want the child exposed to instability.
This pattern concerns me.

Patterns were useful. Patterns suggested inevitability.

Soon, screenshots became folders. Folders became systems. Dates mattered. Times mattered. Context mattered, though it was rarely acknowledged.

I found myself rereading messages not to understand them, but to anticipate how they might later be described.

I was no longer responding as myself.

I was responding as a future exhibit.

This was not paranoia.

It was adaptation.

One afternoon, after saving a particularly long exchange, I noticed something unsettling: my hands were shaking.

SHE CALLED MY WIFE PING PONG

Not dramatically. Not visibly. Just enough that I had to set the phone down and wait for my body to remember where it was.

My wife watched from across the room.

"This isn't normal," she said again, firmer this time.

I nodded. Nodding had become my most reliable skill.

That night, I created a document titled *Communication Timeline*. I told myself it was temporary. That once things improved, I would delete it.

I did not delete it.

7

Sleep

Sleep became unreliable.

Not absent. Just fragmented. Like a radio station you can almost tune in but never quite catch.

I fell asleep quickly—exhaustion saw to that—but woke often. Sometimes to the phone vibrating. Sometimes to nothing at all.

At 3:12 a.m., I would wake convinced I had missed something. An accusation. A demand. A moral failure disguised as concern.

My wife slept through most of this. I envied her. Not because she was unaware, but because her nervous system had not been recruited.

In the mornings, she asked how I was.

"Fine," I said.

This was not a lie. Fine had become a category large enough to contain anything.

At work, colleagues commented on my productivity. Stress, it turns out, can be efficient if properly directed. I responded to emails quickly. I anticipated needs. I avoided mistakes.

Home, meanwhile, had become a place of vigilance.

I checked my phone constantly. Before conversations. After conversations. During conversations.

Once, while helping the child with homework, my phone buzzed. I flinched.

The child noticed.

"Is that Mummy?" she asked.

"Yes," I said.

She nodded, as if confirming a hypothesis.

Children collect information quietly. They do not interrupt the experiment.

That night, I lay awake and tried to remember what it felt like not to anticipate explanation. Not to pre-defend my tone. Not to feel accountable for someone else's emotional equilibrium.

The memory felt theoretical.

PART III

THE ADMINISTRATIVE LIFE

8

File Names

The first thing that happened was that my memories began to acquire extensions.

They were no longer just experiences. They were PDFs. PNGs. Time-stamped artifacts stored in folders that multiplied quietly while I slept.

The file names started cautiously.

Messages — March

Messages — April

Neutral. Reasonable. Optimistic.

Then they grew more specific.

Derogatory Language

Threats re: School

Accusations re: Mental Health

This was not escalation. This was taxonomy.

I took no pleasure in this. If anything, I found it faintly humiliating. It felt like admitting failure—not of the relationship, but of imagination. I had reached the point where I needed evidence to convince myself that something was happening.

Zola, meanwhile, continued with admirable consistency.

I just want clarity.

I don't understand why you're being so difficult.

This wouldn't be an issue if you were cooperative.

Cooperative was another word that arrived preloaded.

Cooperative meant alignment.

Alignment meant agreement.

Agreement meant disappearance.

One afternoon, after saving yet another message that read like a polite indictment, I noticed I was narrating my own actions in legal language.

I am responding in good faith.
I am attempting to de-escalate.
I am prioritizing the child.

I sounded like a man applying for parole from his own life.

My wife suggested a different filing system.

"What about dates?" she said. "Timelines make sense to courts."

Courts. The word had entered the house like a distant storm system—still theoretical, but no longer implausible.

That night, I reorganized everything.

Folders within folders. Labels refined. Chaos given the illusion of obedience.

At midnight, I closed my laptop and felt briefly victorious.

This, too, passed.

9

Neutral Language

Neutral language was supposed to help.

This was the advice I received from well-meaning people who had never been trapped inside an argument that regenerated itself automatically.

"Keep it factual," they said.

"Don't engage emotionally."

"Stick to logistics."

So I did.

My messages became models of restraint.

Pickup will be at 3:30 p.m.

I will confirm attendance by Friday.

Please let me know if there are any changes.

Zola responded as if I had insulted her.

Your tone is cold.

This feels dismissive.

I'm trying to communicate and you're shutting me down.

It was at this point that I understood something fundamental:

Neutrality was not neutral.

Neutral language removed what she needed—reaction. Without reaction, she was forced to escalate abstraction.

Now the messages were about *process*.

This dynamic isn't healthy.

I don't feel heard.

I'm worried about long-term impact.

Impact was a flexible concept. It stretched to accommodate anything.

I forwarded one particularly long message to my wife.

She read it twice.

"What does she actually want?" she asked.

This was the question everyone asked. Friends. Family. Me.

SHE CALLED MY WIFE PING PONG

The answer, I was beginning to suspect, was not an outcome.

It was continuation.

As long as the conversation existed, she remained central. As long as she was responding, I was orbiting.

That night, I created a new folder.

Communication Patterns.

The plural mattered.

10

The Bundle

The word *bundle* entered my life quietly.

A lawyer used it casually, the way one might suggest a different brand of coffee.

"You'll need to prepare a bundle," she said.

A bundle, it turned out, was not a thing you gathered. It was a thing you constructed. It implied intention. Order. Narrative.

Until then, I had been collecting. Saving. Archiving. The bundle required something more deliberate: selection.

Selection meant judgment.

This felt dangerous.

Judgment suggested taking a position. Taking a position suggested conflict. Conflict, I had learned, was what I was accused of creating simply by existing.

Still, the idea lodged itself in my mind.

That night, I opened my folders and scrolled slowly, as if entering a museum of my own recent life. Messages that once felt overwhelming now appeared strangely uniform. The same phrases, recycled. The same concerns, rearranged.

I'm worried.
This doesn't feel right.
I need reassurance.

Reassurance was infinite. There was no amount that satisfied it.

I began grouping messages not by date, but by function.

Insinuation.

Accusation.

Threat.

Concern framed as inevitability.

This was not vindictive. It was forensic.

At some point—around 1:30 a.m.—I realized I was calm.

This surprised me.

Outside the immediacy of response, her words lost their momentum. They were no longer arrows. They were artifacts.

By dawn, the bundle existed in outline form.

It felt unreal. Like a prop from a play about my life rather than the thing itself.

When my wife woke, she found me still at the table.

"You okay?" she asked.

"I think so," I said. "I think I understand it now."

This was not optimism.

It was clarity.

11
Translation

Preparing the bundle required translation.

The language of lived experience did not survive intact once introduced to institutions. It had to be converted into something flatter, safer, easier to consume.

She messaged me constantly became *high-frequency communication.*

She insulted my wife became *derogatory references to third parties.*

I felt trapped became *experienced distress.*

Each conversion lost something essential.

Still, I did it.

I wrote summaries. I attached exhibits. I numbered pages.

I avoided adjectives. Adjectives implied emotion. Emotion implied unreliability.

Zola, meanwhile, continued to message.

She did not know about the bundle. Or perhaps she suspected. Either way, her tone shifted again.

Now she sounded wounded.

I don't recognize you anymore.

You've changed.

This feels adversarial.

Adversarial was an accusation that presumed innocence on one side. It was also, I realized, a projection.

The act of documenting had altered the dynamic. She could sense it. The rhythm had changed. The responses were slower. More deliberate.

She sent longer messages.

I sent shorter ones.

For the first time, the imbalance tilted slightly—not in power, but in awareness.

SHE CALLED MY WIFE PING PONG

That night, while saving yet another message that accused me of emotional distance, I felt something close to irony.

Distance, I had learned, was the only safe place.

PART IV

INSTITUTIONS

12

The Building

The building did not look like justice.

This was a disappointment.

It looked like a regional office for something uncontroversial. Licensing, perhaps. Water permits. The kind of place where disputes are resolved with clipboards and patience.

Family Court announced itself only through signage. Modest. Sans-serif. Apologetic.

Inside, the air had been scrubbed of personality. Beige walls. Grey carpet. Chairs arranged to discourage conversation. Everything about the space suggested that feelings were not welcome unless they arrived laminated.

I checked in at the counter.

The clerk did not look up.

"Name," she said.

I gave it.

She typed for a moment, then gestured vaguely toward the seating area.

"Take a seat."

This was not advice.

It was instruction.

I sat.

Around me, people waited with the practiced stillness of travellers who had learned that impatience only prolonged things. Folders rested on laps like pets that might bolt if unattended.

I placed my bundle beside me on the chair.

It looked heavier here.

This amused me briefly. I imagined the pages absorbing institutional gravity, becoming denser simply by proximity.

Across the room, a man argued quietly into his phone about pickup times. A woman stared at the floor with the intensity of someone negotiating internally whether to leave or disappear.

No one made eye contact.

Family Court did not encourage witnesses.

When my name was called, it sounded unfamiliar. As if it belonged to someone else who happened to share my paperwork.

I stood, collected the bundle, and followed the clerk down a corridor lined with identical doors. Each door suggested a smaller version of the same problem.

Inside the courtroom, the bundle was no longer mine.

This was another surprise.

Once placed on the table, it ceased to be a record of lived experience and became an object to be referenced. Cited. Flipped through.

A lawyer summarized its contents in a voice that suggested moderation.

"The parties have experienced ongoing communication difficulties," she said.

Communication difficulties.

I wrote the phrase down in my head, filing it away as something to unpack later.

Zola sat across the room, composed. She did not look at me. She looked at the judge, as if presenting herself for approval.

When she spoke, her voice was calm. Concerned. Measured.

She used many of the same words I had seen in her messages. Tone. Boundaries. Safety. The child's wellbeing.

Hearing them aloud, stripped of context, they sounded reasonable.

This was the danger.

The judge nodded. Lawyers nodded. I nodded reflexively, like someone caught in a group exercise.

When the bundle was referenced, the judge said, "Yes, I've reviewed the messages."

Reviewed.

The word landed oddly.

As if six thousand messages could be skimmed like a restaurant menu. As if volume itself were not the point.

Still, something happened.

SHE CALLED MY WIFE PING PONG

The court slowed the conversation.

Questions were asked. Clarifications requested. Time expanded.

Urgency—Zola's most reliable tool—lost traction here. The building did not respond to it. The building responded to schedules.

By the end of the session, nothing dramatic had occurred. No declarations. No reckonings.

But boundaries had been named.

Communication channels discussed.

Expectations outlined.

Limits implied.

Outside, the sunlight felt unchanged. Cars passed. People ate lunch.

My phone remained silent.

For the first time, I considered the possibility that interruption, not resolution, might be enough.

13

Orders Pending

The phrase *orders pending* followed me home.

It sounded provisional, almost polite, like a rain forecast that wasn't ready to commit. Still, it changed the temperature of things.

Zola messaged that evening.

I hope you're reflecting on today.

This process doesn't need to be adversarial.

We both want what's best.

Best had become a word without content. It functioned the way packaging does—bright, reassuring, empty.

SHE CALLED MY WIFE PING PONG

I responded briefly. Logistics only. The child's schedule. Neutral tone. No commentary.

She replied twice more. Then three times.

Concern. Hurt. Disappointment.

I did not reply again.

This was new.

It felt unnatural, like holding my breath underwater—not painful yet, but unsustainable. I waited for the familiar tightening in my chest. It did not arrive immediately.

Instead, there was a pause.

A space.

That night, lying beside my wife, I said, "If I don't answer, does that make me cruel?"

She did not answer right away.

"No," she said finally. "It makes you unavailable."

The difference mattered more than I could articulate.

In the following days, the court moved slowly, deliberately. Documents circulated.

Schedules were proposed. Language grew increasingly specific.

Specificity, I learned, was the enemy of manipulation.

Zola's messages became longer, more emotional.

I don't recognize you anymore.
You've become distant.
This feels punitive.

Punitive was an interesting word. It suggested punishment where none had been assigned. It suggested guilt in the absence of conviction.

I did not respond.

This was not discipline.

It was survival.

14

Silence

The silence did not arrive all at once.

It crept in unevenly, like a tide uncertain of permission.

An hour passed without a message.

Then two.

Then an entire afternoon.

I checked my phone compulsively at first. Not out of longing, but habit. My body still expected interruption. My mind still rehearsed explanations.

When none arrived, the absence felt accusatory.

Silence, I had learned, was never neutral. Silence was always read.

But this silence was different.

It was not performative. It was enforced.

Orders arrived by email a week later. Unadorned. Impersonal. Precise.

Communication restricted.

Channels defined.

Conduct restrained.

I read them sitting at the kitchen table. The same table where I helped the child with spelling words. The same table where messages had arrived like weather warnings.

And then—nothing.

No rebuttal.

No late-night clarification.

No emotional appendix.

The quiet was so complete it felt artificial.

That evening, I cooked dinner without interruption. My wife spoke without pausing mid-sentence. The child laughed loudly, unselfconsciously.

Later, brushing my teeth, I noticed my jaw was unclenched.

SHE CALLED MY WIFE PING PONG

I stared at my reflection, suspicious.
This was not peace.
It was absence.
But absence, I would learn, was a beginning.

PART V
THE WITNESSES

15

Parents

My parents experienced the saga as a long-distance event.

This was partly geographical and partly philosophical. They came from a time when problems were solved by endurance and silence, preferably in that order. Emotional complexity was something you tolerated privately. Legal language was something you avoided if at all possible.

My mother asked about practical things.

"Are you eating properly?"

"Is the child sleeping?"

"Do you need me to make soup?"

Soup, in her worldview, was a universal solvent. It fixed illness, grief, and moral confusion with equal efficiency.

My father listened.

This was his primary method of engagement.

He had lived through enough history to mistrust drama. He believed strongly that time revealed truth, and that patience—while uncomfortable—was preferable to confrontation.

Still, even he had noticed the phone.

He noticed the way I checked it reflexively.

The way conversations paused when it lit up.

The way my posture shifted slightly, as if bracing.

Once, while we were walking together, it buzzed. I stopped mid-step.

He said nothing.

But later, he said, "You don't have to answer everything."

This was his version of a manifesto.

SHE CALLED MY WIFE PING PONG

When the court orders came, my mother cried.

Not because of victory.

Not because of vindication.

Because something had finally stopped moving.

My father nodded once.

"That makes sense," he said.

This, from him, was thunderous approval.

16

Siblings

My siblings processed things differently.

They joked.

This was not cruelty. It was proximity. Humour allowed them to stay close without being pulled under.

"She's really committed to the bit," one of them said, scrolling through a sample message I had shown them.

"Does she get paid per paragraph?" another asked.

At first, the jokes were welcome. They lightened the room. They suggested the situation was survivable.

SHE CALLED MY WIFE PING PONG

Over time, the jokes slowed.

They began to notice patterns.

The way my answers grew shorter.

The way I flinched at interruptions.

The way I narrated my own actions pre-emptively.

They learned the vocabulary without meaning to.

Orders.

Timelines.

Communication protocols.

One of them said, "This feels... structured."

It was meant as a joke.

It wasn't wrong.

After the silence settled, they noticed something else.

I stayed present longer.

I laughed without checking the room.

I stopped explaining myself.

Families don't always know how to intervene. But they are experts at noticing change.

At a gathering months later, one of them said quietly, "You seem taller."

I laughed.
But I understood.

PART VI

AFTERMATH

17

Muscle Memory

The first thing I noticed was my shoulders.

They had been raised for so long that lowering them felt like a decision rather than a reflex. I caught myself holding tension in places that no longer served a purpose, like furniture arranged for guests who had stopped visiting.

Violence leaves muscle memory.

This was not something anyone told me. There were no pamphlets. No checklists. Just the sensation of bracing for impact that never arrived.

I still checked my phone too often.

SHE CALLED MY WIFE PING PONG

Still anticipated interruption.

Still rehearsed explanations before speaking.

My wife noticed before I did.

"You don't need to justify that," she said one evening, after I explained—unprompted—why I was late to dinner.

"Oh," I said.

I had been explaining myself to rooms that were no longer hostile.

At work, colleagues remarked on my calm. This amused me. Calm, I had learned, was often just exhaustion disguised as professionalism.

The silence held.

This surprised me daily.

18

The Child

Children do not need closure.

They need consistency.

This was something I learned slowly, watching the child move through the quiet like someone testing new furniture. She spoke more freely. She interrupted. She argued about trivial things with appropriate enthusiasm.

She no longer watched my face when my phone vibrated.

One afternoon, while drawing, she said, "It's quieter now."

"Yes," I said.

"I like it," she added, and returned to her work.

That was all.

There was no grand conversation. No processing. No explanation.

The nervous system, it turned out, did not require narrative. It required safety.

I felt a wave of guilt then—not sharp, but persistent.

Guilt for having normalized something that should never have been normal. Guilt for having waited. Guilt for having believed that endurance was the same thing as virtue.

But guilt, too, softened in the quiet.

I was learning that repair did not require perfection. It required presence.

19

Identity Without Urgency

The problem with urgency is that it gives you a job.

For six years, my job had been responsiveness. Availability. Calibration. I had become very good at it. Excellent, even. I could read subtext faster than most people read headlines. I could anticipate dissatisfaction before it arrived. I could draft apologies that sounded sincere without conceding anything concrete.

This skill set was suddenly useless.

SHE CALLED MY WIFE PING PONG

Without the noise, I discovered large stretches of time with no instructions. No moral tests disguised as logistics. No requirement to be "on."

This should have felt liberating.

Instead, it felt like unemployment.

I woke earlier than necessary. Checked my phone reflexively. Opened emails that did not require my attention. I hovered at the edge of conversations, waiting for escalation that never came.

My wife noticed.

"You don't have to earn peace," she said, watching me reorganize the pantry for the third time in a week.

I nodded. Then I reorganized it alphabetically.

Absurdity reveals itself quietly. It doesn't announce itself. It waits until you're folding towels and suddenly realize you're doing it with the intensity of someone defusing a bomb.

The absence of crisis revealed how much of my identity had been shaped by managing it.

Who was I when no one was disappointed in me?

The question lingered longer than I liked.

20

Grief

No one had warned me about the grief.

Not the obvious kind. Not grief for the relationship—that had been processed slowly, thoroughly, bureaucratically.

This was grief for the person I had been while surviving.

There was a strange intimacy in vigilance. A sense of purpose. A clarity that came from knowing exactly what not to do. When the threat disappeared, so did the certainty.

I missed the predictability of chaos.

This realization embarrassed me.

It felt disloyal to relief.

But grief does not negotiate. It arrives where it is not invited.

One afternoon, walking alone, I felt it sharply—a loss not of what had happened, but of the version of myself who had learned to endure it. That man had been precise. Controlled. Tireless.

He had kept the child safe.

He had kept the house running.

He had survived.

And now he was no longer required.

I let him go slowly.

That evening, I sat with my wife without speaking. No phones. No agenda.

She took my hand.

We did not discuss anything.

This, I realized, was also communication.

PART VII

CLOSING

21

Ping-Pong Revisited

Years later, the word still surfaced occasionally.

Ping-pong.

It appeared unexpectedly, the way childhood jingles do, or the name of a street you once lived on. It carried no heat anymore. No charge. Just the faint outline of something that had once been significant.

At the time, I had believed the insult itself was the violence.

I had been wrong.

The violence was not the sentence.

The violence was the expectation that I would engage with it.

SHE CALLED MY WIFE PING PONG

Ping-pong is not a game about winning. It is a game about continuation. The ball exists only as long as two people agree to keep it moving. There is no progress. No conclusion. Just momentum.

For six years, I had been the other paddle.

Every reply had kept the ball alive.

Every clarification had sent it back across the table.

Every attempt at reason had extended the game.

The insult had been incidental. A flourish. A reminder of access.

When the court imposed silence, it did not side with anyone. It did something far more radical.

It let the ball fall.

No one cheered.

No one conceded.

Gravity simply resumed its job.

The child does not remember the insult.

This feels important.

She remembers other things: quieter mornings, dinners without interruption, adults who finished sentences. She remembers that the house stopped bracing itself.

This is how I know the game is truly over.

22

The Last Message

There was no last message.

This is unsatisfying, narratively. People expect final texts. Closure. A neatly phrased acknowledgment of wrongdoing.

None arrived.

Instead, there was a day when I noticed I had not thought about her at all. Not while making coffee. Not while answering emails. Not while listening to the child talk for five minutes about something that mattered deeply to her and not at all to anyone else.

This, it turns out, is how these things end.

Not with reconciliation.

Not with justice.
Not with understanding.
They end with attention redirected.
I keep my phone face-up now.
It does not frighten me.
Sometimes it vibrates for ordinary reasons.
Sometimes it doesn't vibrate at all.
I no longer narrate myself.
I no longer anticipate tone.
I no longer explain silence.
The furniture remains.
The house breathes.

If violence once entered quietly, it left the same way—without announcement, without ceremony, without asking to be remembered.

That is its final insult.

And also, finally, its defeat.

Author's Note

This book is a work of literary nonfiction written in the form of a novel. Identifying details have been altered to protect privacy, particularly that of a child. The narrative is not an argument, nor a legal account. It is an attempt to describe coercive control as it appears in ordinary life—through repetition, urgency, abstraction, and systems that struggle to name harm that leaves no visible marks.

If the story feels restrained, that is intentional. This is how such violence survives: by sounding reasonable, by wearing normalcy, by asking not to be taken too seriously.

Silence, when finally enforced, is not absence.

It is boundary.

Dedication

For the child,
 who noticed everything,
 and for those who learned that silence can be
an act of care.

Epigraph

"What hurts the victim most is not the cruelty of the oppressor, but the silence of the bystander."
— Elie Wiesel, 1968 Nobel Peace Prize winner

Author Bio

Dr Johan Janssen is a retired cardiologist and has published over a hundred peer-reviewed medical articles and contributed to medical books, which is the sort of thing people say in introductions right before you're expected to clap politely. He has also written books and made films for the general public, because heart disease is complicated and people are busy and, anyway, denial is a lifestyle.

He's active in philanthropy and has translated numerous works about the afterlife, which is either reassuring or alarming, depending on what kind of day you're having. In his spare time (a phrase that suggests fantasy), he plays the piano and looks after his bees and chooks. He also has eleven grandchildren, which means he is essentially running a small nation.

He wrote this novel because family and domestic violence has far too many faces, and most of them are still being politely ignored. And as Elie Wiesel made clear, silence is not innocent.

www.ingramcontent.com/pod-product-compliance
Lightning Source LLC
Chambersburg PA
CBHW062042290426
44109CB00026B/2701